THE PUSSE

THE PUSSERS COOK BOOK

The Pussers Cook Book (*Revised 2019*)

THE

PUSSERS

COOK BOOK

Revised edition 2019

TRADITIONAL ROYAL NAVY RECIPES

INCLUDING BABIES HEADS, CHEESE USH,

CHEESY-HAMMY-EGGY, POT MESS &

SHIT-ON-A-RAFT

Confirmed
not stolen
from the..

The Royal Navy, known as the 'Senior Service', is the longest established British armed force. It officially became the 'Royal' Navy in 1660.

Over the following hundreds of years, the Royal Navy developed countless traditions, official and unofficial; one of these is the development of its own vernacular language, commonly known as 'Jackspeak'.

As we all recognise, the common language of a British Sailor is often colourful. For reasons of authenticity, I have not shied away from using the terms, jargon and slang current during the period these recipes would have been regularly on the ship's menus during the 1960s to 1980s.

While not considered 'politically correct' terminology nowadays, 'Jack' would have simply said, "Rammit, I'm RDP".

Therefore, they have been incorporated in **'The Pussers Cook Book'** as a record of factual historical significance.

Paul 'Knocker' White

THE PUSSERS COOK BOOK

CONTENTS

Cooks at work in the galley of a Royal Navy ship
during the Malta convoys.

21 August 1942.

Before we start on the recipes for all the amazing scran you have missed since leaving the mob, I shall list on the following pages many of the prime ingredients every ex-matelot should have in their homes galley's store.

This is not intended to be a comprehensive list of stores, simply a guide to many of the ingredients which you will need to re-create these wonderful Naval dishes.

<<< >>>

The Naval names for these foodstuffs are in **Bold** text, followed by a Civilian description in *Italics*, for ease of translation to the uninitiated.

Admiralty ham... *Spam*

Arries. Also known as **Arry's** and **Comanche Bollocks....** *Tinned Tomatoes*

Black coated workers.... *Tinned stewed Prunes.*

Bullets.... *Pussers Marrowfat peas.*

Bum Nuts... *Eggs* (NOTE: often referred to as **Crackleberries** when boiled.)

Burgoo... *Oatmeal Porridge.*

B.I.T.S. Beans in tomato sauce...*Baked Beans.*

Cow Juice... *Milk*

Corned Dog... *Corned beef.* (More usually it was Corned Mutton. But who could tell!)

Growler... *Pork Pie.*

H.I.T.S... *Herrings in tomato sauce.* Tinned.

Gammies... An older expression, meaning *Raisins.*

Khai. (Kai & Kye)... *Hard block Chocolate.* Later used to refer to any cocoa based hot chocolate drink.

Limers... *Pussers lime crystals.*

Niggers Dick... *Black Pudding.*

Nutty... *Sweets/chocolate* (of any description.)

Periscope cheese... *Tinned processed Cheese.* (An older expression.)

Pixey Pillows... *Ravioli.*

POM... *Instant Mashed Potato powder.* (Became a generic name for all processed mashed potato.)

Redders... *Tomato sauce/Ketchup.*

Sembawang Sausage... *Satay* from Singapore.

Slide... *Butter.*

Spithead Pheasant... *Kippers.*

Stickies... *The collective name for any & all buns, cakes etc.*

Thickers *1... Condensed Milk.*

Thickers 2 ... *Cornflour and Bisto.* In fact, any agent that can thicken gravy and sauces etc.

Tot... *Pussers Rum.* A mainstay for **ALL** home kitchens.

Snorkers. Also **Snags**... *Sausages.*

Whales... *Tinned Fish.* (any type.)

<<< >>>

There are possibly many more items I have forgotten over the years, maybe I shall remember them or be informed of them after this book is published.

But for now, I think this is a good starting list to base any home Galley's store upon.

Happy cooking, shippers

Can Spanner

We are almost ready to cast off.

There are just a few more terms to get to grips with before we can put our steaming bats on and get underway.

The following are common naval terms when referencing food, although they are not necessarily the names of any food item.

<<< >>>

Ballerina shit... *Pink Blancmange.*

Banyan... *Picnic. (Preferably on a beach somewhere hot and exotic)*

Bun Fight... *Tea party. Usually ashore with the ladies.*

Big Eats... *A slap-up feast. Often ashore on pay-day or simply grabbing something to eat, often late at night after a good sesh, when on the way back to your ship.*

Can Spanner... *Tin opener.*

Chinese Wedding Cake... *Rice Pudding with currants or raisins in it.* (This is also known as Japanese Rice Pudding & Niggers in the Snow.)

Chokey Nosh... *Any Chinese/oriental(style) food.*

Choke & Spew... (Often miss-termed as Choke & Puke). *Originally a café near HMS Tamar in the 1960s.* Now an all-encompassing name for any Greasy spoon café.

Clacker... sometimes Clakker, Clagger or Awning. *Pastry of any type.*

Cock & Arse party... *Cocktail party.*

Cowboys Meal... *Bacon and beans.*

Eating Irons. (Grappling Irons)... *Cutlery.*

Four O'clockers... *Tea-Time. Commonly sarnies and stickies.*

Floaters in the Snow... *Sausage and mash.*

Gipper/Gyppa/Jipper... *Any gravy.* (Also, any stock/liquid for/from cooking.)

Labradors Arsehole... *Sausage Roll* (Look 'end on' and imagine!)

Mess Medals... S*tains & debris down the front of a jumper*, jacket etc. caused by spilt food or drinks. Frequently collected when eating egg Banjos.

Mystery bag... *Meat pie* (often of unknown content.)

NATO Standard... *Tea (or Coffee) with Milk & two sugars.*

Nine O'Clockers... *Late scran/supper.* Often sandwiches and stickies.

Oggies… *Cornish Pasties.*

Pussers Terrapin… *A rectangular pie* with any, (often unknown), filling.

Ring Stinger… *Extra Hot Curry or Chilli.*

Shit & Periods… *Sausages with tinned Arries.*

Sick/Baby sick… *Sandwich spread.*

Snaffle/Yaffle. To *stuff one's face* with food. Often too quickly, in great quantity, or both.

Tiddy Oggies… *Like Oggies only smaller.*

Yellow Peril… *Smoked Haddock.* (Usually accompanied by a poached egg.)

LET'S SET SAIL WITH SOMETHING SIMPLE.

BITS

BEANS IN TOMATO SAUCE.

(Commonly known as Baked Beans.)

'*Unbeanknown*' to many, the history of the Baked Bean is global, from South America to France and England; from where sailors took the humble bean back across the Atlantic Ocean, but this time to some place called Boston, in North America.

Did you know…the now common tinned, or canned, Baked Bean, first arrived in the UK from American companies in 1886 and was sold in the Fortnum & Mason store in London as an expensive foreign delicacy?

To make your own authentic Baked Beans you will need:

Fat Bacon or Salt Pork.

1 large Onion. 3 sticks Celery. (Both roughly chopped.)

4 Cloves.

4 tins chopped Arries (Tomatoes.)

Molasses or Black Treacle (and maybe some brown sugar.)

Black Pepper, Salt.

and of course, some beans....

Okay, so how do you make a Brahma of a Baked Bean?

Like this....

The first thing you need is a heap of beans; 'Navy Beans' sometimes called White Beans or Haricot Beans. If you want to get all technical, the Latin designation is Phaseolus vulgaris.

So, go get around 2lbs of these little babies and put them in a large pot. Cover them with cold water and leave them alone while you go and get your Big Zeds.

In the morning strain the Beans and ditch the old 'Oggin.

Cover with fresh water, and chuck in a small handful of salt, about enough to fill your palm, should do the trick. On medium heat bring the Beans to a boil and then turn the heat down and let them simmer away. While your Beans are cooking, you need some Bacon or Cured Pork, something slightly fatty is the best. I like to use Smoked Streaky bacon. Don't get the thinly sliced stuff from the supermarket, it is full of water and tastes like the inside of a steaming boot.

Ask a Butcher to slice an inch/inch and a half thick piece. He may even chop it into small one-inch chunks for you. No need to be too precise about it. If you can't get any bacon, use some Speck, (cured pork.)

Toss the diced Bacon into a pan with a good heavy bottom, one like the 44's on the Gronk board. Pile in the 4 Cloves, chopped Onion and the chopped sticks of Celery. Fry off until onions are soft and Bacon beginning to brown.

Drain the cooked Beans and add them to the heavy-bottomed pot with the Pork, Onions & Celery. Add the tins of chopped Arries.

Dollop in the Black Treacle or Molasses. *(If you cannot find either of these, use Soft Brown Sugar, but it is NOT the same.)* You will need about 4 to 5 oz. That's 8 to 10 tablespoons full.

Some people add a sprinkle of Mustard at this stage. *(I don't.)*

Sprinkle in a couple of pinches of Black Pepper. Mix it all together and put a lid on. Make sure the lid fits tightly.

Place pan in the oven and bake at about 250F/130C/gas mark ½ for about 8to 10 hours.

YES. It is all worth it.

These will be the Bessie Beans in the whole world.

Once done you can play about with the recipe, adding garlic, Tomato puree? Or even a Tot or two?

Try it out.

Have fun.

Cheese Ush can be made with a clacker base, as a flan of sorts, or without any clacker at all.

The choice is yours.

I prefer it with a clacker base, so with that in mind, I include the pasty here.

But if you want it without, just leave it out.

Instead, line your baking tray with two layers of well-greased, greaseproof paper, or if you are modernised, line the dish with parchment paper... (*newish stuff, they never had it in my day, but the wife swears by it.*)

As for the clacker, you can buy it from any local slops like Aldi, Tesco or Waitrose. It comes on a roll 'ready rolled' if you are a right lazy sod or in a block, which will need rolling out.

Alternatively, you can ask the missus to knock you some up, or if you're feeling energetic, have a go yourself.

Here is how you make a basic shortcrust pastry.

Get all the stuff you'll need together; clear all the junk off the worktop and then sieve 8oz of plain flour and a pinch of salt into a large bowl in the centre of the cleared area.

Put another half-handful of flour on a small plate or saucer near the big bowl.

Place a saucer with 4oz of unsalted butter on the side next to the bowl. Make sure the butter is as cold as it can be.

Half fill a cup/mug or Jug with cold water. Set that on the workbench too.

Have some table salt within reach.

It will help if you have a knife and a fork. A set of eating irons is perfect.

This is what to do next.

Using the knife, roughly dice the cold butter into small, (½ inch) cubes, letting them fall into the flour in the big bowl as you cut them, or toss them in by hand after cutting. Either way works.

Begin rubbing the butter and flour between your fingertips, just the tips, so the heat from your hands does not warm the mix too much.

The best way is to grab some flour and a cube of the butter, suspending your hands a few inches above the bowl, rub them together like you would if calling a cat towards you.

Keep doing this over and again until the entire bowlful resembles breadcrumbs.

Now start adding the water, a VERY little at a time, mixing it as you go. DON'T get it too wet. If you are unsure, go to the next step, you can add more dribbles of water as you go.

This is where, at least at the beginning, you may want to use the other eating iron (*fork*) in a sort of mixing/spoon-stirring fashion until the mix gets too sticky, then revert to the hand job.

To stop the clacker sticking to your fingers dust your fingers with the extra flour you put to one side on that saucer earlier.

Once the mixture resembles something like putty you are there.

Stop mixing, form it into a rough ball shape, cover with cling film and pop it in the fridge.

You just have plenty of time for a decent cuppa before making the Ush.

This is the Cheese Ush bit.

You ONLY need to do this bit if you are going without the pastry base. Why you wouldn't want your Ush sat on clacker I have no idea, but I have heard some weirdo's like it that way. (Probably some Airy-Fairy two-ringer.)

Anyway, you will need.

Cheese, grated. (Cheddar, Red Leicester, Double Gloucester are all suitable.) A block of Pussers Cheddar is traditional, but I like some Red Leicester mixed with it.

You will need around ½ a pound to 10 oz.

A finely sliced or chopped medium sized onion.

Two or three eggs, dependant on how big the buggers are and some squashed Arries, (tomato puree), a small can or one of those squeezy tubes. Up to you, it's all the same shite inside.

Oh, and a drop or two of Worcestershire sauce.

If you are using Clacker, get the chilled ball from the fridge, using the rest of the flour from the small plate, dust the surface and rolling pin.

Roll out the clacker until it is large enough to cover the base and sides of the dish you are using.

TIP: Loosely roll the whole lot around the rolling pin and lift it over the dish, slowly unroll, allowing the pastry to settle onto the dish.

With your fingers, gently but firmly press the pastry into the corners and the sides of the dish, trying not to get any air pockets. Trim off any excess hanging over the edges.

Set this aside to wait for the Ush to be ready.

Making the Ush

You really need a mixer for this, but you can do it by hand.

Chuck the grated cheese and chopped onion into a bowl and set the mixer going. Use a LOW speed.

As it mixes, squirt in some tomato puree to make it a

deeper orangy-red colour and give it a splash of Worcestershire sauce.

Keep mixing, you can probably turn the machine to a slightly higher speed now.

Add the eggs in, one at a time. (*NO shells, just to be clear),* letting each one mix-in well before adding the next.

After the last egg has been added, let it mix for another minute, the stop the beater.

The Ush is now ready; pour/scoop into your pastry.

garnish with a few tomato slices, if you want to faff about, and bake in a moderate oven.

That's something around 350f/180c/gas mark 4. It should take about half to three-quarter of an hour (or so).

Check at twenty-five minutes and so on. You are looking for a 'puffed-up', slightly risen Ush with a golden-brown top.

Stick a cocktail stick into the centre if you're unsure. If it comes out 'clean' you should be about there. If not cook for another few minutes. (*You can also check by prising the middle apart a bit and taking a shuftie.*)

That's it.

Cheese Ush, done.

A LITTLE NOTE ABOUT FOOD.

CORNED DOG

The First Mention of "**Corned Beef**" goes back to an English Book by Richard Burton in 1621, '*Anatomy of Melancholy... Beef... corned young of an ox.*'

The date 888 AD and the term 'corned' can be found in the Oxford English dictionary.

It had long been discovered meat did not rot as quickly if is it was in contact with enough salt over a long period.

'Corns' is the name used to describe the large grains of rock salt which are used to preserve meat.

Hence the name 'Corned'. It simply means 'Salted'.

The nitrates contained is the corns converted the natural haemoglobin into methaemoglobin, which leads to giving salt-preserved meats a pink colour.

It is also accepted the nitrates reduce the risk of botulism during curing. Often beef cured with only salt takes on a shade of grey. During modern manufacture spices and sugars are often added for flavour and extra preservation.

One point which is important is that 'Corned Beef' is a form of salted beef and can be found as joints of meat. The Jewish dish *'loof'* is one such.

The more common version of Corned Beef, that which comes in a tin or can is a rather more modern. An industrial affair, beginning around the time of the industrial revolution when canning of food helped its preservation when supplying armies and the fleet.

Nowadays, corned beef is a prime inclusion of the worlds armed forces ration packs because of its stability and ease of preparation. *(None necessarily needed, simply open the pack and eat.)*

It may still surprise many Matelots much of the Corned Dog consumed by the Royal Navy 1970-1980s was not beef at all, but Corned Mutton.

Now you know.

THE PUSSERS COOK BOOK

Babies Heads is one dish which almost every sailor I have spoken to mentions.

I doubt if anyone can, or will ever, replicate the strange form of clacker coating the original tinned puddings the Royal Navy acquired back in the heydays of the '60s & '70s.

Even the well-known brand of steak & kidney puddings sitting on most supermarket shelves cannot hope to cast a shadow upon those wonderful tinned victuals from the Pussers store.

The best we can do now is to prepare and cook our own versions.

BABIES HEADS

By keeping to traditional recipes and following age-old methods the resultant Puddings should be a joy to eat.

Whichever version of Babies heads you decide to try, the Suet Clacker is the same, so **here is that recipe.**

(You can make this while the filling is bubbling away on the stove.)

Butter, for greasing

285g/10oz self-raising flour

125g/4½oz suet

1 tsp baking powder.

Pinch of salt.

If you wish you can add some dried or chopped herbs to the Clacker. Parsley and Savoury both work well with Babies Heads.

Generously butter a 1.2 litre/2-pint pudding basin

Mix the ingredients together and season with salt and pepper.

Gradually stir in water until you have a soft, slightly sticky dough. *(You will need about 225ml/8fl oz of water)*

Take about a quarter of the dough, to be used for the

pastry li put it to one side.

Dust your work surface with flour and roll out the larger piece of dough into a circle roughly 30cm/12in in diameter. Use this to line the pudding basin, leaving the excess pastry hanging over the edge. Roll out the small piece of dough you set aside until it is large enough to form a lid for the basin.

For the filling:

30g/10 oz. unsalted butter.

vegetable oil, for frying.

2/3 Onions, chopped.

2 garlic cloves sliced/crushed.

1 tbsp. plain flour.

1 tbsp. finely chopped fresh rosemary or savoury.

500g/1lb-ish Beef. About 1" diced. (I like to use Shin, but if you prefer more 'bite' to your meat try rump.)

salt and freshly ground black pepper.

3 lamb or ox kidneys. Remove the core and any other tendrils. Dice.

150ml/5fl oz. red wine/brown ale/porter. (Your choice.)

150ml/5fl oz. rich beef stock.

Melt the butter with one tablespoon of oil in a large,

heavy-based fanny over medium-low heat.

When the butter is foaming, chuck the onions and garlic into the pan, cook for a few minutes until they begin to soften.

Meanwhile, in a large bowl, mix the tablespoon of flour with the chopped herbs and some salt and pepper. Add the lamb and kidneys and toss them thoroughly in the seasoned flour.

Transfer the onions and garlic to a large bowl and set to one side. Add a little more oil to the pan and increase the heat.

Add a third of the lamb and kidney and cook until browned all over.

Set aside with the shallots and repeat with the remaining meat, adding more oil if needed.

Do the same with the beef.

Chuck everything you have cooked in batches back into the big fanny.

Add the wine and or beer to the pan, bring it to the boil for a couple of minutes.

Scrape the base of the pan with a spatula/wooden spoon to help release any caramelised bits.

Add the stock and simmer for five minutes. If the sauce looks too thick, add a little more stock. Taste the sauce and season with salt and pepper.

Set aside to cool. You cannot add hot filling to cold clacker...it will melt!

Spoon the cooled filling into the pastry-lined basin.

"Scran will be late! We've lost the ruddy tin opener!"

Dampen the edges of the overhanging clacker with water.

Put the lid on, pressings the edges together with the one you have just dampened, this will make a firm seal which will, hopefully, keep all the gubbins firmly inside. Trim away any excess.

Place a piece of greaseproof/baking parchment over a sheet of foil and make a large pleat in the middle, folding both sheets together. Place, greaseproof side to down, over the pudding, *(this allows the pudding to expand as it cooks)*. Secure with string. Tie it around the 'neck' of the bowl to do so, looping the end of the string over the top of the pudding and tying it to form a handle that will enable you to lift the pudding in and out of the boiling water in the fanny.

(A muslin pudding cover would be best, but there are not many of these about nowadays.)

Place the basin in the big fanny and pour in enough boiling water to come halfway up the side of the basin.

Cover the fanny with a lid and bring it to a simmer.

Turn the heat low and let the pudding steam for 2-2½ hours.

Top up with boiling water as needed.

DO NOT let the pan boil dry.

Eventually, you can remove the pudding from the pan, take off the foil and parchment and leave to rest for five minutes.

(It is at this stage you can, if you wish, make a small hole in the top of the pudding and add oysters, stirring them well into the pudding through the hole. Be careful not to touch/damage the puddings wall or it will collapse when turned out.)

Personally, I think oysters in a Baby's Head is wrong, but then each to their own.

Use a small, sharp knife to release the sides of the pudding from the basin. Put a large plate over the pudding and invert it, so the pudding comes out on to the plate.

Serve straight away.

Guinness or a tot always works well as an accompaniment.

Then... There is always a BABIES HEAD cake.

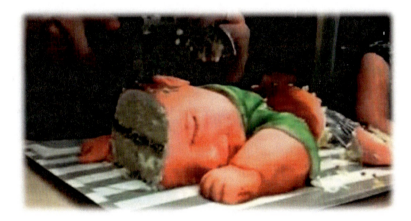

BURGOO

This is the name of ships porridge. Hence a Scotsman is known as a Surgoo-eater.

(Okay, don't ask)

For each person, you will need around half a pint of Rolled oats.

A couple of cups of water. (*This may be substituted for milk or made up Millac)*

Two(ish) dollops of butter. (*about tablespoon size,* optional) The same amount of sugar.

Slowly pour the water onto the oats, stirring all the time until well mixed.

Bring to the boil over medium heat, stirring frequently to stop it from catching on the base of the saucepan.

One boiling away, reduce the heat and let it simmer, stirring occasionally. When oats are becoming tender add sugar and butter. You can also add some salt if you wish.

Stir until all is well mixed and oats are smooth and tender.

That's it.

31

THE PUSSERS COOK BOOK

CHEESY-HAMMY EGGY

I know you are slavering as you read this, it is the effect this dish has on anyone who has ever tried it.

Historically, this is the Royal Navy's take on the classic French 'Croque Madame'... but who really gives a shiny shite about that?

Here are two ways to make Cheesy-Hammy-Eggy, a simple and relatively quick way and the *'cooks own mess version'*.

Guess which I prefer?

Version No.1

Take four slices of white bread.

Four slices of sliced ham. (More if you are thinking about using that wafer-thin stuff...please don't, use real ham.)

Five eggs.

¼ pound, that's about 125g, of Cheese.

A teaspoon of English mustard.

Method.

Mix together the cheese, mustard and one egg.

Grill one side of your bread (all four slices.)

Place half toasted bread uncooked side up and cover with ham.

Cover with cheese mix spread to the edges.

Pop under the grill while you fry off the remaining four eggs.

Pull cheese-hammy out from under grill when golden and bubbly, (or when eggs are cooked enough for your taste.)

Place one egg on each cheesy-hammy. You now have basic

cheesy-hammy-eggy.

Version No.2

(For four slices, as above)

¼ pound/125g grated cheddar cheese.

Four slices of good ham, or enough shreds to cover the four slices of bread. (Yorkshire or Lincolnshire dry-cured ham works well.)

About a teaspoon of mustard. English does the job, but a good wholegrain works too. *(I have one with beer and whiskey in it...Mmmmm).*

A few splashes of Worcestershire sauce.

Five eggs.

(Nine... if you like double eggy hammy's?)

Four slices of bread. (*Sliced, packaged bread is okay, but for that real 'Jack's Galley' style try making some or buying a split-tin loaf from a bakery. Cut it into inch thick slices.*)

Mix cheese, mustard, Worcester sauce and egg together to form a thick-ish paste. (*Whisk the egg and add it a little at a time until you get the right consistency.*)

Toast all four slices, but ONLY one side.

On the uncooked side of the half-toasted bread put a good layer of ham, double layer if you are peckish.

Cover the ham with the Cheesy mix, smoothing it over

with a pallet knife, if you know what one is, works well.

Place all four cheesy covered ham slices of bread under the grill while you fry-off the four eggs. I like to cook mine, in pure unsalted English farm butter, on a lowish heat.

When eggs are cooked and cheesy mix golden and dripping hot, place cheesy-hammys on a plate and top each with one (or two) of those fried eggs.

THAT is how to recreate a true Naval sensation.

CHOKEY NOSH

(Sometimes, wrongly referred to as Chogie/Choggy Nosh)

This is a term used to describe any Asian influenced foods. Chinese/Thai/Korean/Japanese etc.

Real Jack was never so prissy as to warrant varying definitions of regional scran.

Chokey Nosh is an all-encompassing term which suits its purpose and is understood by all concerned, regardless of the meal's true identity.

On-board Chokey Nosh was as wide and varied as:

1 The ingredients available.

2 The Cooks experience.

3 The Cooks temperament.

4 The Cooks sobriety.

5 The Sea conditions.

6 That last one is bullshit. Just seeing if you're paying attention.

There were, however, a few rules that had to be adhered to for the dish to be classed/recognised as Chokey Nosh.

Firstly, it had to contain Beansprouts. Always from a can.

The same goes for the Water Chestnuts and Bamboo Shoots. (*occasionally canned Baby Sweetcorn would be available*)

Along with the above, the dish would have to have: Shredded Cabbage or some form of Greens. *(Possibly florets of Cauliflower or Broccoli if fresh.)*

Thinly sliced onions, baton or sliced carrots and any other vegetable that could be stir-fried.

NOTE: For 'stir fry' read pan-fried or dry fried.

Chunks of canned Pineapple were often a key ingredient.

Noodles and/or Rice were always cooked to accompany a Chokey Nosh. Plain boiled or fried.

Once again it very much depended on what the cook could be arsed to do that mealtime.

To flavour the said Chokey Nosh, there were again a set of key ingredients. These flavourings could be utilised in any number of combinations to produce something which vaguely reflected an Asian or Far Eastern taste. *(At least if you had a good imagination.)*

The key flavourings were: Soy Sauce, Tomato Puree, Ground Ginger, Pepper, Honey and Salt. Plus, any spice nicked from the bakery cook. *(Who was more than likely getting his head down as he was on duty again at 03:00hrs)* like Nutmeg, Allspice, Cloves, Cinnamon etc.

Once this lot was 'stir-fried' together and swamped with soy sauce the dish was complete.

Chokey Nosh, al la Naval Cook, (jnr.)

THE PUSSERS COOK BOOK

EGG BANJO

In fact, any Banjo. Bacon and Egg Banjo. Snorkers and Arries with fried Egg Banjo.

ANY bloody Banjo at all.

Banjos are bread rolls; preferably submarine rolls with sunny side up fried eggs (*or assorted omelettes*) as the filling.

Originally bought by matelots when returning from a run ashore in Singers.

One of these oversized sandwiches was big enough to

provide your supper, the remains frequently devoured as breakfast following morning.

It is the common belief the Banjo got its name because the egg yolks would split when the sandwich was bitten into, the yolks dripping down the front of jumpers and jackets causing an array of mess medals to form.

To prevent this, the diner would hold the sandwich up in the air with one hand, while trying to wipe away the stains on his clothing with the other.

This action, when seen by onlookers, looked vaguely like the diner was playing an *'Air Banjo'*.

Whilst this is common belief and has been accepted by many as part of the 'Banjo' legend, it is **TOTALLY WRONG**.

The term 'Banjo', when referring to an overfilled submarine sandwich, has been around (*at least),* since the First World War.

The origination of the term comes from a song by Andrew Barton (Banjo) Paterson (1864-1941), poet, solicitor, journalist, war correspondent and soldier.

He was born on 17 February 1864 at Narrambla near Orange, New South Wales, Australia.

This is Banjo Paterson's song/poem

I love my egg filled sandwiches

As I sit here in the sun,

Sometimes from a loaf or

Even in a bun.

I love when the egg runs down my chin

And my mates think it's a joke,

I look in a nearby mirror

And I'm covered in its yolk.

What could I call my sandwich,

A word that will be in history?

I know what I'll do mate,

I'll name it after me.

Mmmmmmm, my egg filled sandwich

See the juices start to flow,

I love my egg filled sandwich

My lovely Egg Banjo.........

As for a recipe for a Banjo... Don't wind me up.... just slam
anything you fancy into a soft white submarine roll and

top off with two, or three, or four lightly, sunny-side-up, fried eggs.

It really IS that simple.

Andrew 'Banjo' Patterson

ELEPHANTS FOOTPRINTS

Also, known as Nellie's Wellie's, are simply Spam Fritters.

You Need

1 x 340g can SPAM® (Chopped Pork and Ham... allegedly)

150g x plain flour.

225ml x cold water.

Oil for frying.

Cut SPAM into six thick slices.

Put most of the flour into a mixing bowl, (*keeping a little in reserve for coating the Spam before dipping into batter mix)*

Gradually add the cold water, whisking continuously, until the mixture is fully blended and smooth. *(It needs to be quite a thick, coating batter)*

Heat the oil in a large frying pan.

Dip each slice of SPAM into the reserved flour and then into the batter. Allow any excess to drain off.

Immediately place the coated spam in the hot oil fry until golden brown. *(The batter should be crisp.)*

Lift from hot oil with tongs or spatula and place on kitchen paper to drain off excess oil.

Serve with chips, peas and a good glug of redders.

NOTE: Besides the 'original' Spam you can now get Spam 'Light', Spam with 'Real' Bacon?

Other options are purchasing your Spam in an 'Easy open tub', a plastic affair, rather than a tin/can.

For those who are lazy or totally inept in a galley you can also buy ready-made Spam fritters, ready-coated in a 'Crispy, golden batter'.

I kid you not.

Jinga Moli

This is clearly the Pussers derivative of Jhinga Molee, which is a South Indian preparation.

The main ingredient is cooked in rich coconut milk; it is also used in Sri Lanka and among Malays.

It is often called 'white curry'.

The Coconut milk, being the main ingredient, makes it deliciously mild. When cooking, the pan must not be covered at any time. The liquid should be stirred while coming to the boil to prevent curdling.

Casting aside all traditional recipes and methods, this is the Main Galley's version, whittled down to suit a family of four-ish rather than an entire ships company.

Ingredients:

500g Prawns or 3-4 small tins (If fresh, which is best. Peel, devein and rinse in clean water before using)

1 tbs Peanut Oil or, as I prefer Ghee. (We had never even heard of Ghee in my day!)

2/3 Thin sliced onions

3 finely chopped garlic cloves. Or some paste from a jar.)

2 Red or green chillies, cut into very thin strips. (Whimps con remove the seeds/ or use a hot chilli paste.)

1 tsp Ground turmeric

8 Curry Leaves. *(Another ingredient we never had. Bog standard curry powder, madras hot, was what we used. So, for an RN classic, go for that option. I still do.)*

1 tbs grated fresh root ginger. (Or a good dollop of paste from a jar.)

600ml Coconut Milk.

1 tbs Lemon Juice.

1-2 tbs chopped fresh Coriander.

NOTE:

Traditionally, lamb or chicken is often combined with prawns to make the meal more substantial. To keep it seafood(y) the addition of lobster or crab meat works well. *(NOT traditionally Navy, but worth a try.)*

Grab a large fanny and stick it on the heat. A big wok does the job too.

Heat oil and fry off the onions until translucent, chuck in the spices (Garlic, chilli, curry leaves, turmeric). Toss it about for a few seconds and then add the coconut milk.

Be sure to stir frequently as you bring the mix to the boil. Once bubbling, turn the heat down and allow to simmer for 10 mins. Chuck the Prawns in.

If using fresh prawns, once the jipper is back up to heat, allow to simmer away for around 8 minutes.

If using canned ones, once back to simmering cook for only 3 minutes.

Season (*salt & pepper.*)

Remove fanny from the hob. Squeeze on the lemon juice and scatter chopped coriander on top.

Serve with plain boiled or Jasmin rice.

Eat.

THE PUSSERS COOK BOOK

KHAI

Pussers hot chocolate.

It is possible the term 'Khai' originates from the Nong Khai region of Thailand, where chocolate is grown.

Khai is victualed as a large dark unsweetened block of chocolate (Cocoa), to be grated when required.

Grate the chocolate from the block into a mug or large pan. Hot water and/or milk is then added and stirred vigorously until well mixed before being drunk.

Sugar can be added if required. It will be, unless…

Often, half a mug of hot, almost boiling water, was used to dissolve the cocoa before condensed milk, (Connie/thickers) was added.

After some time at sea, connie was often the only palatable milk, even after the infamous 'Millac' was introduced.

The use of condensed milk usually made the chocolate sweet enough that adding sugar was unnecessary.

Khai was also prepared in larger quantities for the

watchkeepers. The Khai was grated into a large fanny, water/milk applied and stuck under a steam drain in (*B boiler room*) to boil up.

It was then distributed among the middle watchkeepers.

Blocks of Khai were often scraped with a Pusser's dirk to *'grate or shave'* the hard blocks of cocoa, never mind traces of red lead, grease or another shite that may be on the blade.

According to the old hands, it all added to the flavour.

Stokers used lots of Connie and plenty of sugar whilst going easy on the water. They liked it best when the spoon stood up in the centre of the mug without any support.

One other addition which was frequently used in Khai was a tot or two of Pusser's rum, a dark liquid that tends to make most things taste better.

LIMERS

A strong lime flavoured drink made from lime crystals, sugar and water.

This IS NOT a recipe...but it is well worth reading. (*That's why it's in this book)*

Scurvy is caused by a prolonged deprivation of vitamin C. There are many descriptions of the disease as it appeared among sailors engaged in the long voyages which began to be undertaken from the end of the fifteenth century.

After ten or more weeks at sea, men began to experience general pain and stiffness, while their lower body became covered with large purple spots.

In addition, their gums would swell and grow over their teeth, which became loose; old wounds would reopen. Finally, sufferers would die suddenly, "in the middle of a sentence," to the astonishment of their mates.

The first "antiscorbutic" (*i.e. anti-scurvy*) foods to be prized by sailors were oranges and lemons, but they would become mouldy on long voyages. Juices preserved with brandy or rum were more stable alternatives. They also proved to be more palatable!

Sailors in the British navy were required, from early in the nineteenth century, to take a portion of lime juice in their daily ration of rum; men from other navies called them "limeys" as a term of abuse, implying that "real men" did not need to drink fruit juice.

'Limers' was introduced as a simple way to ensure that a good supply of ascorbic acid (vitamin C) was constantly available onboard Royal Naval ships.

This concoction, however, has created its own legend.

The following are a few genuine dits from 'Jack' regarding the juice...

"In the tropics, we had a bucket of limers in the workshop. It was kept in an old boiler gauge glass; the elongated end was used as a straw. Dozens of people sucked on it each watch, so for hygiene, we would occasionally turn the gauge glass over."

"I recall a POME bringing his motorcycle aboard in pieces, (having been refused permission to bring it on board as an entire machine). During the foreign leg, he completely

refurbished the parts and re-assembled the bike. When we returned to Pompey he wheeled his motorcycle down the gangplank. It was far cleaner and shinier than when it was brand new.

The secret was, he said, dumping the whole engine block in "limers" and leaving it a few days.

"On the Mohawk, we used limers on the upper deck woodwork to get it looking "whiter". Never mind what it did to our guts. We used to brew it in the Buffers Store/Paint Shop. Also, amazing if we had an FFO spillage during a RAS."

"I always thought it a great drink and very refreshing when in the Far Flung. We used to have an ice cold 5-gallon tub constantly on the go in the dining hall of HMS Hampshire in 66/67."

"We used to have a large container of it in the canteen flat, along with a ladle to help yourself. I now live in Cyprus and the temperature at present is 100+ each day? I drink in Gallon.! Pity though it is not the pucker stuff in crystal form that made your teeth clench; nothing in this world is the same anymore, Bloody Politicians, first Rum, then Harry Limers, what next?"

"We used to have the Lime powder mixed in a small bucket ready to drink in the boiler/engine room, that was 68. Didn't last long when out the Far East, we drank it in gallons."

"Anyone noticed that most of the old stokers 'got no teef left' after drinking this highly acidic potion.

HMS Tiger, circa '77.

"Just behind the serving hatch of the main galley, there was a small preparation area. It is here that a three or five-gallon pot brimming with Limers stood, often clinking away because of the amount of ice dumped into the pot (from the Scotsman ice maker from outside the cook's mess/reggies office), to keep it cold for as long as possible.

As the main galley was one of the 'hotter' areas of the ship, we cooks needed to sup gallons of cold limers to keep from dehydrating.

I cannot reveal who, or which Scab Lifter it was, but the cooks had an illicit supply of 'medical' alcohol.

Now that stuff is pure and potent, akin to meths and could easily blind a man.

BUT... when diluted with enough limers in a large pot its potency was kept under control. (sort of)

Besides as we all used the same ladle to drink from, so the addition of alcohol was a hygienic necessity"

'Grogram', by the way, was an early waterproof fabric that Admiral Vernon, nicknamed 'Old Grogram' used to sport.

This nickname was quickly shortened to **'Grog'**.

The rum allowance was a quarter of a pint twice a day *(although the pint measures were then about 20% smaller than now)*

Sailors mixed the rum with brown sugar and lemon or lime juice, then topped it up with water to make 'grog'.

Below, is a so-called 'four water' grog, 4 parts water to 1-part rum.

You can always tighten it up, although once you're in 'two-water' territory you'll quickly find your guests...

"Stupefying their rational qualities, which makes them heedlessly slaves to every passion."

As the good admiral Vernon, Old Grogram himself warned.

But then again, your guests probably don't have ships to command

ADMIRAL VERNON.

LIME GROG

16 ounces lime juice (*or Limers*)

1-pound brown sugar.

1-pint rum – (*dark rum*)

1/2-gallon water.

6 springs mint.

Collins glass.

In a large bowl or jar, mix the fresh-squeezed lime juice and the brown sugar. *(You may want to use less sugar...try starting with 1/2 pound and working your way up)*

Dilute with the water and rum (*use an old-fashioned dark navy rum),* if a 'Pussers' rum is not available, try one from Jamaica, Demerara, Bermuda, or somewhere akin.

Drop in the mint.

Refrigerate and serve on the rocks *(Unless you're a stickler for historical accuracy)*

THE PUSSERS COOK BOOK

POT MESS

This may cause controversy

You see there is no true or 'original' recipe for Pot Mess; it is simply a ships stew made with any available supplies.

Dependent on which foodstuffs were to hand and which cook was responsible for the 'pot' resulted in how the Pot Mess would taste.

It is that simple.

There are two methods of creating an authentic Pot Mess. The first is using fresh ingredients, the second is where almost everything comes out of a tin can.

Pot Mess from a tin

Generally, the canned Pot Mess consisted of Stewed steak.

(Steak from which animal or from what century it was tinned, was never disclosed. The cans never had any labels, just a non-descriptive statement of content stamped on the top).

Tinned potatoes & tinned Carrots roughly chopped, Peas, Swede, Turnip, Broad Beans, Baked Beans, in fact, anything.

If came in a can, it was used.

Luckily, many of these vegetables were ready diced, such as the ubiquitous 'Mixed vegetables.'

The chopping of vegetables for tinned based Pot Mess was often done with a simple table knife, an eating iron, not a cook's knife.

It did not need to be sharp. The method was to 'cup' the

vegetable, say carrot or potato in the palm of your hand and, using the blunt-ish eating iron, cut the article with a downward stroke.

The knife would easily pass through the soft pre-cooked vegetable but stop when it hit the palm.

This way it was possible for two cooks to 'chop' their way through several of those large tins (A4's) in record time.

About the only thing, which was added to this version of Pot Mess, which was not from a tin, was the onions.

These were usually prepped from fresh and sautéed down in a 'copper', (*a large fixed pan with a steam-heated jacket.*)

Once the onions were softened all the other ingredients were chucked in the pot, as and when they were prepared.

The water and/or stock added last.

Flavourings like Redders (Ketchup), Worcester sauce, salt, pepper, garlic, soy sauce, brown sauce and such were added at this stage.

The whole 'Pot' being stirred about with a massive ladle as it simmered away for hours.

Gravy mix, a Bisto type gravy powder and cornflour were used to thicken the Pot Mess nearing the end of cooking.

Pot Mess version two.

(This is the more elusive 'all from fresh' style.)

A large GM tray, or three, of roughly diced 'Chuck & Blade'.

This cut of beef was the usual choice for Pot Mess, although any chunky cut meat, or combinations of meats, including ox heart, scrag end of lamb and corned dog, can and have, been used.

Sometimes the meat would be tossed in seasoned flour and sealed *(fried off until brown)*, sometimes it would just be dumped in a copper along with the vegetables.

These were usually carrots, potato, leek, onions, swede, in fact, all root veggies were considered fair game.

Other additions often added near the end of cooking may be pie fillings, savoury mince or such, possibly left from lunchtime or yesterday's dinner, along with unused vegetables from the same.

The whole lot was boiled for hours with handfuls of dried herbs and the same seasoning agents as used in the tinned version.

Again, powdered gravy mix and/or cornflour, or even potato powder (POM), was used to thicken the Mess towards the end of the cooking process if needed.

Pot Mess originated from 'Lobscouse'.

The word comes from the Norwegian word for stew - 'lapskaus'

(It is the same word that gave native Liverpudlians their nickname of 'Scouse', which they also use to describe an indescribable stew!)

To try to reproduce a traditional Lobscouse you will need:

50g beef dripping

750g shin of beef, cut into rough 2cm cubes

1 large onion, peeled and chopped

3 carrots, peeled and roughly chopped

500g medium potatoes, peeled and quartered

200g dried peas, soaked overnight

A few sprigs of thyme

2 litres beef stock

Salt and freshly ground black pepper

50g pearl barley

Melt the dripping in a heavy-bottomed fanny.

Brown the meat in the oil, remove it from the pan and set

aside.

Then fry off the onions until translucent, even a touch 'golden'. *(A trick here is to add a sprinkle of demerara sugar. This helps the onion to caramelise.)*

Add all the other ingredients, return the meat to the pan and mix together.

Bring the fanny to a boil.

Turn heat down and simmer for around two and a half to three hours. Season with salt and pepper, serve.

SHIT ON A RAFT

This is a dish I am frequently asked about.

A simple search of the internet finds pages and forums asking about **'shit on a raft'.**

It must be one of the most popular of all the long-established dishes.

Without wanting to disappoint all you diehard traditionalists, let me say there is NO hard and fast recipe, no 'cast in stone' method of conjuring up this particular delicacy.

Each ship, even each cook, would have put his own spin on 'shit on a raft' according to the stores available and the mood the cook was in at the time.

Here are two versions, both differ greatly.

The first is my preferred version, the Galley Rats version. The second is for lazy OD's.

If you want to fancy-up your 'Shit on a Raft' try piping some POM around the edges of the toast.

This will help keep your Shit on the Raft.

In the Bunhouse, Shit on a Raft was often described on the meat chit as **"Excreta a-la Kon Tiki".**

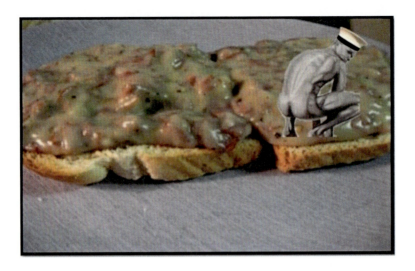

You will need a handful or two of Kidneys. That's about a 1lb or 8 – 12 according to size.

Lambs kidneys are the traditional navy fare. They used to come in frozen slabs in huge boxes. Pigs kidneys are great too.

1 Medium onion chopped *(Peel it first).* Optional, but makes it taste even better.

1 Tablespoon of flour

1 heaped teaspoon of mustard, or half teaspoon mustard powder.

The 'Proper' yellow English mustard, not the gnat-piss French stuff.

Add a squirt or spoonful of Tomato Puree. I have known some to add Redders, that's fine.

A cup of water.

That's half a mug for you Stokers. But you might want a bit more. You can add it if needed.

Chicken, or beef stock cube, or OXO. *(Unless you have homemade stock, then use that.)*

A teaspoon of Cornflour on standby. *(Just in case it is not thick enough, or you added too much water.)*

Pepper and salt.

Bessie Method.

Fry onions until translucent.

Quarter Kidneys (removing core and any crap)

Toss in seasoned flour. (the kidneys, not yourself)

Fry for 3 - 4 minutes. Turning as they cook.

Chuck everything not yet used into the pan with the onions & kidneys, simmer for 3(ish) more minutes.

Do all this in one frying pan.

Serve on a fried bread 'raft'.

OD's Method.

Take the kidneys.

Chuck them into a saucepan of cold water

Bring to the boil and simmer for about 10 minutes, or until tender.

Thicken the liquid with Bisto (or your preferred gravy mix.)

Serve on fried bread.

COOKS TIP.

Posh it up. Pipe some POM around the edge of the fried bread, this not only looks good but stops the shit from falling off the raft.

HARRY SKINTERS.

This is a step further than shit on a raft.

At Portland, it was called SAUSAGE TURBIGO and was fantastic for breakfast, lunch or tea.

Make enough, so after your evening meal you can have it warmed up on toast as an 'anytime snack'.

Grab a dozen lambs' kidneys, leave the rest of the lamb to 'carry on'.

Clean them (*the kidneys not the lambs*) and cut into small pieces discarding all the white cores/tubes and sinews.

Dump them in a pan of cold water, add an oxo cube (*There are other stock cubes available. Use any make you choose.*)

Season with (*freshly ground*) black pepper.

Finely chop an onion and fry gently for a few minutes to

soften. Add to pan with kidneys. Gently simmer for about 10 minutes until tender.

Bung in some sliced mushrooms you should have prepared earlier.

Thicken the liquid if required with some cornflour, or Bisto gravy powder. *(Other gravy powders are…. oh hell, you've read that bit before.)*

While all the above is going on, you'll need to fry or grill a handful of Snorkers.

Once nicely browned chops said Snorkers into bite-sized pieces and chuck 'em in the pot with everything else.

Stir about a bit.

When the kidneys have cooked through enough for you to enjoy, the entire dish will be ready for you to scoff at leisure.

Enjoy.

Another great classic. Rich meaty filling, flaky 'rough-puff' clacker.

You will need:

2lb of blade-bone steak (Other cuts can be used such as sirloin or rib-eye...it's up to you)

2 kidneys.

1 large onion.

2/3 Bay leaves, some thyme.

1 tablespoon flour (*Cornflour if you prefer*)

Black Pepper and salt.

Can of Strong Dark Ale or some of that Black Stuff from Ireland.

SNAKE & PIGMY

PIE

Bisto on standby.

The Clacker you prepared earlier and is chilling in the fridge.

Remove most of the fat from the meat, all the thick big bits anyway. Don't be too fussy after that.

Cut the beef into cubes, about 1/2" square.

Remove skin from the kidneys (*essential*) along with the tubes and any other white bits.

DITCH all these unwanted bits over the side. The fish love them.

Cut the kidneys into small pieces as you have the meat.

Heat some cooking oil in a skillet (*frying pan.*)

NOW... roll your beef in the flour to coat it and shake off excess.

Put several cubes of your flour coated beef chinks into the pan and fry until the flour turns brownish.

Remove your meat from the pan and slip it into a large fanny. Repeat until all your beef is browned-off.

Now add the kidney and onion to the fanny, along with your beef, pop in two or three bay leaves, a palm-full of dried thyme, or a couple of small bunches if it is fresh thyme.

Pour the beer or Irish porter over the lot & top up with cold water if needed, until liquid is about level with the gubbinns.

Mix the flour or cornflour in a cup into a paste with cold water.

(You add this to the pot nearer the end of cooking, as It is the thickening agent.)

Season with pepper and salt.

Bring to boil then allow to simmer gently for 1 1/2 hours, or till meat is tender and the stock reduced to a nice even gravy.

If it is too thin, 'runny' add the thickeners (Cornflour) or some Bisto type gravy thickening agent.

Only add a small amount at a time and allow it to 'cook out', (thicken the mix) before adding more. Once you have the consistency you desire, adjust seasoning (salt & pepper), to suit your taste buds.

Have a well-greased (with butter) pie dish, lined with the clacker from the fridge.

(*You can also buy clacker readymade and even rolled out... what will they think of next?*)

Bung filling into pie dish and brush around the edge of the clacker with egg wash. (B*eaten egg let down with a little water or milk.*)

This will help the pie's lid stick to the top pastry and stop all that 'luverly' filling from oozing out.

Cover with more clacker, press onto eggy part of lower clacker to form a seal and pinch the two parts together. The technical term for that is 'Crimping'.

Or you can squash it down with the tines of a fork.

Trim the rough edges of clacker around the dish edges to stop the raggedy bit burning.

Brush over with remaining egg wash.

Stab the lid in two places to form small holes. This allows the steam to escape as the pie heats up and will stop it exploding in your oven.

Bake in the oven until pastry is golden brown.

About 30/45 minutes should do it.

Another original Royal Naval term for a dish with no 'correct' recipe.

Train Crash is, as the name suggests, is a wreck of food heaped onto a plate.

This was one dish which helped the catering officer balance out the Pussers food budget.

Quite simply, Train Crash was the unused ingredients from breakfast recycled into a form of Pot Mess for lunch or dinner.

There may have been one or two other ingredients added from time to time, but substantially it was chopped up and mixed together English breakfast.

Bacon cut across the rasher into strips, Sausages sliced, Baked Beans, Spaghetti, Comanche Bollocks (chopped), Re-fried 'sautéed' potatoes, crumbled Black Pudding and so on.

Occasionally some kidneys or Corned Beef might find its way into the crash.

That is, it. A simple dish which can be easily replicated at home.

Simply make it up as you go along, we did.

YELLOW PERIL

Smoked haddock with a poached egg.

A fish kettle is perfect for this, but a shallow skillet or frying pan works too. All the better if it has a well-fitting lid.

In the pan put half water half milk to a level so it just covers the thickness of the fish by about half an inch. (*That's 2.5mm, or so I am told*).

Add a bay leaf, three black peppercorns (plus pink corn or two if you have them), a couple of thin slices of onion and a clove.

Place fish, skin side down (*on the trivet if using a fish fanny.*) Add a knob of unsalted slide to each piece of fish.

Cover pan with lid, or a layer of greaseproof and then a layer of kitchen foil, crimping it around the pan to seal in the heat and steam.

Slowly bring to a boil, turn down to a simmer for five minutes and then turn the heat off.

Now, have a saucepan of boiling water & add a splash of malt vinegar into the water, stir it in a circular motion to create a central vortex.

Crack an egg into that vortex. You are now poaching an egg like a chef.

It will only take two minutes or so for the egg to cook. While it is, lift out your Yellow Peril, a fish slice would be useful for this job.

Pop it onto your plate.

Now the egg should be cooked.

Lift it out with a slotted or holed spoon so any excess water drains away and put the egg on top of your fish.

You are now done.

No meal would be complete without something on the sweet side after the main course, especially for a hard-working salty seadog.

The odd bar of nutty was okay in the mess on a night while watching a Shitkicker, a True-Blue or a Micky Duck, but it could not hit the spot for a real sugar rush.

All Pussers puddings come under the term of Duff, Figgy Duff, Sticky duff, Plumb duff, Spotty duff... it was all simply duff.

Even when the 'missus' became pregnant it was never 'a bun in the oven', it was always 'up the Duff'.

The following pages are dedicated to some of the most loved

'Duffs'

Treating yourself to a

MANCHESTER
TART

First, make your own shortcrust pastry or buy some from the local supermarket.

You can even get it ready rolled if you're feeling really lazy.

You will also need some milk, about a pint, 3 tablespoons full of custard powder, a teaspoon of vanilla extract, or half a teaspoon of vanilla essence, or the seeds scraped from half a fresh vanilla pod. A jar of jam, Strawberry is traditional.

Then you'll need about 5 tablespoons of desiccated

coconut and about 4 of caster sugar. Also, a 24cm baking tin. A whisk and a saucepan.

Line a 24cm round baking tin with pastry.

Prick the base with a fork. Lay a sheet of baking parchment on top and top with dried beans. Bake in preheated oven for 20 minutes. Remove the beans and baking parchment and let cool.

Meanwhile, make the custard.

Place milk, custard powder, 2 tablespoons sugar and vanilla extract into a pan, stir until smooth and gently heat until thick. Set aside to cool slightly.

Spread jam over the pastry case and sprinkle with half the coconut. Pour in custard, sprinkle with coconut and remaining sugar.

Chill until ready to serve. (Both the tart and the cook.)

DUFF

DUFF No.1

This is the most basic navy Duff I could find.

Mix together the same proportions of flour and suet.

Add half that quantity of fruit, with some spice, (*nutmeg, cinnamon, clove, allspice…whatever you must hand*).

Squeeze in the juice from a lemon or two.

Splash in a tot drop of rum. (Optional.)

Then one beaten egg and a drop of milk.

It should make an excellent pudding if boiled for a long time.

DUFF no.2

250g pitted dates, chopped. That's dates with the stones taken out. You can do this yourself but it's laborious and ultimately sticky.

1 teaspoon bicarbonate of soda

1 1/2 cups boiling water

125g butter softened

1 cup brown sugar (Soft brown is best, but light brown will do. Use demerara at a push.)

1 teaspoon vanilla extract

2 eggs

1 3/4 cups White Wings Self-Raising Flour, sifted.

For the Caramel sauce, you need...

1 cup brown sugar

300ml thickened cream

1/2 teaspoon vanilla extract

60g butter

Get your oven hot, something around 180°C will do.

Butter a 7cm deep, 22cm (*base*) cake pan. Line it with greaseproof paper. Butter this too.

Place dates and bicarbonate of soda into a bowl. Pour over boiling water. Allow to stand for 20 minutes.

Then..

Using an electric mixer, beat the butter, sugar and vanilla until pale and creamy. (*It takes quite a while. Don't rush it, be patient.*)

Add eggs, 1 at a time, beating each one into the mix in turn.

Drain the dates you have been soaking, discard the 'oggin. Chuck the dates into the butter mix and fold through with a big spoon until well mixed.

The next bit is...

Spoon that mix into the prepared cake pan. *(The one you have buttered and lined.)*

Bake for 35 to 40 minutes. (*Or until a skewer inserted into the centre comes out clean.*)

When it does, turn the baked Duff onto a plate.

To Make the sauce *(You can/should do this while the Duff is cooking.)*

Tip the sugar, cream, butter and vanilla into a saucepan on medium heat.

Cook, stirring almost continuously until it comes to the boil.

Turn heat down until its medium-low. Simmer for another 2 minutes or so.

Last bit...

Pierce pudding all over with a skewer.

Pour 1/2 cup of the hot caramel sauce over the warm pudding.

Allow to stand for 10 minutes before heaping a pile into a bowl and covering with the unused half of the caramel sauce.

Of course, you can share this with up to three other people if you so wish.

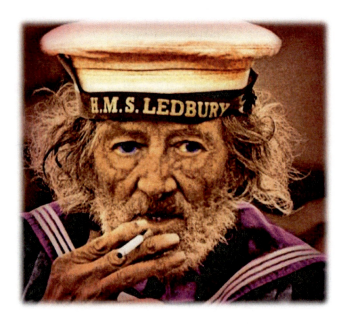

Unless you are really old school, you may not recognise this version of Navy Duff.

DUFF No.3

You will need...

3 cups fresh breadcrumbs, 1 cup raisins

1/2 cup brown sugar, 1 teaspoon ground ginger

1 teaspoon allspice, 1 teaspoon cinnamon

1/2 cup molasses, 1/4 cup melted butter

1 teaspoon baking soda, 1 tablespoon hot water

1/2 cup plain flour.

This is what to do...

Soak the breadcrumbs in water for a few minutes. Squeeze out the water. Put the soggy breadcrumbs in a large mixing bowl with the raisins, sugar and spices. Mix the lot together with a fork.

Pour the hot water over the baking soda and add it to the breadcrumb mix. Now add the molasses (black treacle) and the melted butter. Add the plain flour & mix it all together.

Next step is...

Pour the mixture into a large, well-greased pudding bowl.

Cover with buttered greaseproof paper and a double layer of kitchen foil, (*to keep any water and steam out*). Now secure with an elastic band or some tightly tied string.

Place the pudding bowl - gently- into a large fanny of boiling water. The water should be 3/4 way up the sides of the pudding bowl. (*Any higher and you risk flooding the Duff. Any lower and you could boil dry.*)

Boil away for about 1 1/2 hours so that the Duff steam cooks.

'Really' old school stuff.

PRINCESS FRITTERS

Who could possibly forget the ubiquitous Princess Fritters?

These are, quite simply, a jam sandwich deep fired. Something the Scottish members of the ships company welcomed with open arms, well, mouths to be accurate.

These are so simple to make there is no 'recipe' required, just a simple explanation.

Here is that explanation;

Butter (or not) two slices of bread.

Medium thickness, ready sliced, processed crap will do, but 'real' bread from a bakery or anything homemade is preferable.

Spread each slice, one side only, with a jam of your choice.

Raspberry or Strawberry jams work well, but the stuff Pussers supplied was a plain tin with the legend, 'mixed fruit jam' stamped on the lid.

Lightly press the two slices of bread together, jammy sides together.

Cut the crusts off if you wish, or, if you want curly hair, leave them on.

Slice the sandwiched bread in half diagonally and then

slice each into half again so you end up with four small triangular dainty jam sandwiches.

Repeat this process until you have the required number of sandwiches.

Then mix a basic batter, flour, water, a little backing powder etc. Ensure your batter is thick enough to coat you finger when you dip it into the mix. If it is, you are good to go.

> **COOKS TIP:**
>
> Add a little custard powder to make your batter a more 'golden colour' and to add a hint of vanilla.

Ensure your deep fat fryer, or chip-pan, is up to temperature, around 175 to 180 is ideal.

Dip each small triangular sandwich into the batter, coating it thoroughly.

Gently place it into the hot oil. Repeat with the other sandwiches, but do not overfill your fryer, leave enough room to turn each sandwich over so it cooks evenly on both sides.

You are looking for a 'golden brown' colour but remember when you lift them out they will continue to get darker, only about two shade though, not 50 shades.

While they are cooking pour some sugar into a shallow tray.

Vanilla sugar, even pink coloured sugar, can be used, but the good old white stuff is works fine, although granulated can be a bit gritty, so caster sugar is better.

Once your fried sandwiches are a nice golden-brown lift them out, allowing the oils to drain off, then dump them in the sugar on your tray and toss them around until the sugar is sticking evenly all over the batter.

You have now made the traditional Pussers Princess Fritter.

Serve with custard, yellow or pink, your choice.

This is a great thing to do with your kids/grandchildren by the way…. I mean deep frying the sandwiches, not the children.

There are many more dishes which helped to feed the Royal Navy. But the ones here, in the **Pussers Cook Book** are probably the most famous, (*or infamous*) of them all.

To finalise, I shall leave you with some memories from old shippers, about the other food consumed in great quantities by Jack.

Otherwise known as **BIG EATS.**

*Satay dipped in sauce from a galvanised bucket sold by street vendors outside **Sembawang dockyard.***

The "can you get it all in burger" from the wagon opposite **Pompey** station on a Sunday night. Always good after the carnage of the train journey from **Guzz.**

Porky's Ribs at the Octagon in Guzz, wake up the next morning and the cabin looked like a scene from Texas Chainsaw Massacre.

Seem to remember an Oggie wagon on the **Guzz** side of the chain ferry back in the early '70s! No idea if it's still there or gone when the Old King died.

*Double sausage and a runny egg in crusts, Dot's bus at **Dryad.***

Meat pie wagon opposite Aggies in **Pompey** run by father and daughter, her norks were like Chesty Morgan's... We had her down our mess one Saturday afternoon but that is... I'll say no more.

Rosyth Dockyard '84\5, Glasgow in drydock. Used to go to Jackie O's in Kirkcaldy on a Thursday night, back on board around 03\0400. The civvy canteen was just by the drydock and you could get a full breakfast for not a lot. Comfort food.

Always remember **Malta**, a night down the **Gut** (Hop Leaf or Marsovin) followed by a fried egg banjo from the Dreadnought Bar at Customs House Steps before getting a Dhaisa back across to St Angelo where the **Rusty B** nearly always moored up.

Greasy Spoon at Portland just up from the Shutters - my first experience of the "Messy Burger". Can't remember if they were good or bad, but they didn't blow the guts apart in the morning. Unlike anything from Iranian Ali's burger van in Pompey. Served from that little shack on wheels opposite the RC Cathedral next to the mini roundabout, you were practically guaranteed 15 mins in the shitter before turning to the next day.

Best big eats after a run ashore were at **HMS Fulmer** better known as **Lossiemouth**.

The chefs were given permission to run a Fish & Chip racket from the JRs galley. Fairly priced and the best fish & chips in the area.

I was just thinking the Dreadnought Bar *(complete with hot and cold running cockies up the walls)* in Floriana .. steak banjo's then a Dhaisa back to the ship on the trot in the middle of the grand harbour.

Sembawang *in the mid-80s, the Kiwi's had taken over and seem to remember a place in the married patch that did a mean chilli fried crab.*

Tatties in **Gib** (*later became Mokhtars*) "Chicken on a Fist".

A bag full of Monkeys Bums at the Piazza. (Squid Rings)
Gib.

"Grand memories and grand times, lads. I hope you enjoy this book and try some of the old scran.

Let me know how you get on"

ABOUT THE AUTHOR

Paul 'Knocker' White was a six-week wonder boy who joined Raleigh in 1973. Followed by the obligatory part 2 training at the catering school, HMS Pembroke, Chatham.

His first' real' draft was to Dryad, as a baby chef in the Wardroom, which was an amazing eye-opener as he got to look after HRH Prince Charles, who was then wearing the rings of a sub-lieutenant.

There was also a frequency of other high-level visitors, such as Princess Margaret and the (then) Prime minister, Edward Heath, along with many other dignitaries and their accompanying staff, ensembles & Special Branch security.

For a young boy, just turned 16-years old it is an experience he will never forget.

Paul's first sea draft came by way of a swap draft.

Looking back, it was rather unbelievable for a sprog, junior cook class 2, as he was at the time, to be accepted as a swap for a recently married killick chef who wanted to stay shore based with his (new) wife. Clearly a big love job... Paul wonders if it lasted?

Anyway, good fortune smiled on him and he ended up as wardroom chef on HMS Tiger, the Admirals flagship of the fleet.

Paul never looked back from that day on.

OTHER ROYAL NAVY BOOKS BY PAUL WHITE

HMS Tiger - Chronicles of the last big cat

(Outsized Hardcover. Only available via the author's website)

The Pussers Cook Book

(Paperback & Hardcover. A special eBook version has been published. The hardcover only via the author's website)

Jack's Dits – Tall tales from the Mess

(Paperback)

The Andrew, Jack & Jenny

(Paperback)

Neptune and the Pollywogs

(Paperback & eBook. Released in May 2019. This book is in conjunction with the Royal Navy Research Archives.)

To see all of Paul White's books, fiction and non-fiction, please visit the author's website.

https://paulznewpostbox.wixsite.com/paul-white

Made in United States
North Haven, CT
16 December 2022

29180331R00062